T0348276

Dallas Wínmar
ALIWA!

CURRENCY PRESS, SYDNEY

CURRENCY MINI DRAMAS

First published in 2002
by Currency Press Pty Ltd,
Gadigal Land, PO Box 2287, Strawberry Hills, NSW, 2012,
Australia enquiries@currency.com.au
www.currency.com.au

Reprinted 2015, 2016, 2019, 2023

Set by Dean Nottle.
Cover design by Kate Florance.
Printed by Fineline Print+Copy Services, St Peters, NSW.

Currency Press acknowledges the Traditional Owners of
the Country on which we live and work. We pay our
respects to all Aboriginal and Torres Strait Islander
Elders, past and present.

Publication of this title was
assisted by the Commonwealth
Government through the Australia
Council, its arts funding and
advisory body.

A catalogue record for this
book is available from the
National Library of Australia

Aliwah! was first produced by Yirra Yaakin
Noongar Theatre at the Subiaco Theatre, Perth, on
26 July 2000, with the following cast:

Mum / Alice, **Dot, Reserve Boy**	Rachael Maza
Judith, **School Teacher**	Irma Woods
Ethel, Native **Welfare Officer**	Kylie Farmer

Director, Lynette Narkle
Designer, Tish Oldham
Sound and original music, David Milroy
Lighting Designer, Mark Howett

Playwright's Note

Aliwa is a play made up of many layers.

It is a journey through past and present.
It is a journey through old and young.
It is a journey from father's death to mother's death.
It is a journey from father's grave to mother's grave.
It is layered with letters from the native welfare files.
It combines narration with dialogue.

It is a play about survival, dignity and strength.
It is a play about a mother trying to keep her family together when policies of the time tried to break them up.

It is a form of story telling.

Some people don't believe that things like this ever happened in the past.
That every Aboriginal family had a file on them.
Or that the assimilation policy ever existed.

It is just one story told to me, and there are so many more stories to tell about this time in history.

It is a story of the hardships of survival and the celebrations of it.

What is important is that our stories be told.
Through the Arts we can now voice and express the stories that make us who we are today.

Dallas Winmar

*I wish to dedicate this book to
Dot Collard,
Ethel Abdullah (deceased),
Judith Wilkes (deceased),
Cecil Winmar (my dad – deceased),
Lily Penny (my grandmother – deceased),
friends and family.*

Characters and Production

The performance was conceived to be played by three actors, Aunty Dot Collard, Frankie J. Bropho and two music men.

The actor who played **Dot** played **Young Dot**, **Old Dot**, **Mrs Pivot** and **Mrs Crawford**.

The actor who played **Ethel** played **Young Ethel**, **Old Ethel** and the **Teacher**.

The actor who played **Jude** played **Mum**, **Old Jude**, **Giddeon**, **Eddy** and the **Cowboy**.

All three were on stage throughout, in the background and working props.

Aunty Dot sat and watched from the sidelines, chucking in her words now and then.

The two music men played the **Boys**, one of the music men played the **Station Master**, **Frankie J. Bropho** played himself (a music man) and **Aunty Dot** played herself.

Mum and Jude read her and Alice's letters, and one of the music men read Mr Neville's letters.

Special thanks to: Yirra Yaakin and staff, Company B and staff, Stages, Neil Armfield, David Milroy, Wesley, Jodie, Liz Doyle, Anna, Wei Han, Alison, Mark Howett, Annika, Wayne, Robert, Ryan, Rachel, Nigel, Chris, Kevin, Ursula Yovich, Trish Morten-Thomas, Polly Low, Louise Gough, Tai, Evonne, Lisa, Lizzy, Dianne, Myra, Alta, Candy, Nick, Robert, Adrian, Yibiyung, Aggie, Deda, O'Sharn and Zane.

ACT ONE

Prologue

Three girls enter the stage and are ready to start.

Jude All I wanted was some facts and details.

Aunty Dot enters.

Ethel You shouldn't 'ave got them, Jude.

Aunty Dot Hey, hey, hey, you lot. Don't go startin' yet.

The girls stop and look at Aunty Dot. They do a silent apology or reaction.

All Sorry, Aunty Dot!

Aunty Dot I've got to tell this mob here what this is all about. This is a play about me and my two sisters. We were going call this play *The Three Sisters*—I heard this Russian guy stole that one. Anyway, this play is about the Davis family. And how we grew up in Western Australia. Don't want to give too much away but. Ningali, come here, come on, come on. This one here, Ningali Lawford, she's from Fitzroy Crossing. She'll be playing my baby sister Jude, and when we go back in the past, she'll be my mother.

Ningali kisses Aunty Dot on the cheek and takes up her position.

Good luck.

Deb is keen. She smiles and starts to walk over to Aunty Dot.

Deb, not you, Kylie's next.

She motions to Kylie.

This is Kylie Belling from Melbourne, and she will be playing my older sister Ethel. All right, that'll do!

Kylie kisses Aunty Dot and takes up her position.

Now, Deb, come here, bub, I'm ready for you now. This is Deborah Mailman from Mount Isa. How can I say this? [*Pause.*] She'll be playing me… They could have got me to play me, but I haven't won no… [*turning to the audience*] AFI Award. Have I? Hope that don't confuse you mob.

Aunty Dot turns and kissed Deb. Deb takes up her position.

[*Turning her back to Deb*] I got my eye on you. Over here is Wayne Freer from Melbourne. And Frankie J. Bropho from Perth, he's a Noongar like me. Now if you are wondering, I'm just here to keep things on track. I'll be sittin' up there with my heater, just watching. Don't mind me, I'll just keep to myself, I won't get in the way. I'll also be watching that director, what's his name, Neil Armstrong. He chucked every trick in the book in this one. Including me!

Aunty Dot sits.

Well. What you three doing? Don't keep this mob waiting. The play will start now.

Jude's House (the present)

Jude All I wanted was some facts and details.

Ethel You shouldn't of got them, Jude.

Jude Why not? It's our history.

Ethel No it's not. That's Wadjella way.

Jude I didn't realise you'd get this upset about it.

Dot grabs files out of Jude's hands.

Dot Where did you get them from anyway?

Jude Family and Children Services.

Dot Arggh! F and Cs.

Ethel All you had to do was ask me.

Jude I just wanted to know about our family, that's all.

Dot Most of it is lies anyway. [*Pause.*] Just bloody lies.

Jude Well, you two don't have to read them.

Ethel Don't worry, I won't.

Jude I thought it would be all right.

Dot Well, it's not.

Jude But at least it gives dates of where the family was.

Dot Like a criminal. Where you went. Who you married. Where you lived.

Ethel It's a disgrace to think that they kept a file on every Aboriginal family. An absolute disgrace.

Dot Just look at the cover. 'Chief Secretary's Department, Aborigines. Subject: Half-caste family of Yarloop: Personal file.'

Ethel Half-caste!

Dot Half-caste, quarter-caste, quadroon baboon.

Ethel Dot, it's not funny.

Dot I know it's not. [*Pause.*] What I want to know is how they measure blood.

Ethel It's like saying my arms are white and my legs are black.

Jude It's not just the government documents. Mum's own letters are in here too.

Ethel I don't want to know about them.

Ethel sits next to Aunty Dot.

Jude Like I said, you don't have to.

Pause.

Ethel What I know is right in here.

4

Ethel points to her head.

Jude Eth, come on, just take a look.

Ethel I'll take a look all right. I'll take them outside and burn them.

Jude It's all right for you, you're older, you've got your memories.

Ethel And I'm holding onto them. That's what I've been trying to tell ya. I don't need them bloody files to tell me what I know.

Jude And that's what I've been trying to tell you. I do!

Pause.

Dot Hey, youse two. Why don't we all go back to Yarloop and show Jude where we grew up.

Ethel Youse two can go.

Ethel exits offstage but is in listening range to hear what Jude and Dot are saying. Dot is aware of this.

Jude I know nothing about Dad. I don't even know where he is buried.

Dot Aye, don't worry, she'll come around.

Jude If youse don't want to come I'll go by myself.

Dot Don't be silly. [*Saying it so Ethel can hear her, but not making it obvious*] Hey, Eth, what year did we move to Yarloop?

Ethel [*offstage, calling*] Why don't you look in them bloody files?

Dot [*whispering*] Aye, sis, put them files away.

Jude [*shouting offstage to Ethel*] I'm putting them files away.

Dot [*loud, so Ethel can hear*] Aye, old girl, come and have a cuppa.

Jude [*loud, so Ethel can hear*] I've got some Tim Tams.

Ethel [*offstage*] Go on. [Gaarn] You can't con me with biscuits.

Dot Come on then. Tell us a few yarns about Yarloop, eh.

Jude How did Mum and Dad end up there?

Ethel [*offstage*] What I know you'll never find in those files.

Ethel enters and sits down.

Orright then. Where's the Tim Tams?

Jude You know what, they come in fingers now. But I couldn't get any from the shop.

The actors improvise about Tim Tams.

Aunty Dot Aye, you lot, shut up about the Tim Tams and get on with the show!

Travelling to Yarloop (the past)

Ethel [*narration*] We travelled from a place called Waroona. Down south-west to Yarloop, a timbermill town. On a wagon hauled by two big dray horses. My sister Dot and I rode on the wagon with Mum, because we were the smallest. While the older boys and girls followed behind with our dog Ruffy. It was loaded with all our worldly goods. We were not rich by any means, but we had plenty of love in our family.

Aunty Dot That was true, unna.

Dot Mum, tell Ethel to stop pullin' my hair, she's hurtin' me.

Mum Ethel! You want to get out and walk with the boys…

Dot Na, na, na, na, na.

Mum Dorothy!

Ethel Mum.

Mum Yes, Ethel.

Ethel Ohh, Mum…

> *Ethel whispers into her mother's ear about going to the toilet.*

Mum Just hop off and catch us up.

Ethel But, Mum, it's moving.

Mum Ethel, we're not going that fast.

Dot Mum, I'm hungry.

Mum Orright, orright, orright, then.

Mum stops the wagon and Ethel gets off.

Ethel, bring some wood back with you, so I can boil the billy.

Dot Where's Dad?

Mum He's gone on up ahead.

Dot How far do we have to go now, Mum, before we get to Yarloop?

Mum Not far, just a couple more hours.

Dot What we got to eat?

Mum Depends on what the boys catch.

Dot Can I go see if they got anything?

Mum Whatever you like—just stop asking questions. And watch where you're steppin'.

Mum is getting the mugs and billy ready. Ethel returns with wood in her arms.

Ethel Those boys are sure having fun with their shanghais.

Mum Have they got anything?

Ethel Six parrots, one rabbit.

Dot Owww.

Ethel And Dot.

Aunty Dot And those boys sure were crack shots.

Ethel [*narration*] By gee, it was a long trip, a sort of adventure, being so young. At that last stop Mum made sure we were well presented. It was like preparing for battle.

Last Stop (the past)

Ethel [*narration*] Mum lined all us kids up in front of the wagon.

Mum Boys, tuck in your shirts.

Ethel [*narration*] With a damp cloth in one hand…

Dot Ow, you're going to rub my face off.

Ethel [*narration*] And a comb in the other…

Mum Dot, let me comb your hair. Yes, there, you're perfect.

Ethel [*narration*] She inspected each and every one of us.

Mum When we get to town, I want you all to stay close to the wagon. It's really important that you all behave.

Dot Why?

Mum Dad's gone to see a man about a job at the

mill, that's why!

Dot I thought he already had one.

Mum Not yet, it's up to the foreman.

Dot He'll get it. Dad's a good worker.

Mum He's the best.

The Mill (the past)

Ethel [*narration*] We arrived in Yarloop outside the foreman's office.

Dot I can't see him.

Mum He's in there. Talking to the man. Now sit still.

Dot Why is he taking so long?

Mum I don't know. Just keep your fingers crossed.

Dot He'll get it. Dad's bigger and stronger than any of them fellas.

Ethel [*narration*] The sound of the steam-driven mill boomed in our ears and the smell of burning logs and smoke filled the air.

Mum Can you see him yet?

Dot Yeah, here he comes and he's smiling. [*Yelling*] Dad, did you get it?

Mum Dot. Come back here.

Ethel [*narration*] As we rode through town people stopped what they were doing and came out and stared at us as we went by.

Aunty Dot And I bet they wished we kept on going too. The wagon piled high with mattresses, a sewing machine, Mum's best china, eight kids and Ruffy tagging behind. We must of looked like the Beverley Hillbillies, unna.

Dot Those people are staring at us.

Mum Just sit up tall and smile.

Dot [*pointing*] Look. But, Mum, it's rude to stare.

Mum And point.

Ethel [*narration*] The mill supplied houses for all its workers. It might have been Dad who got the job, but it was Mum who chose the house.

Dot Hey, Mum, I like the one with the white picket fence.

Ethel Yeah!

Mum You lot stay here, I'm going to look at this one over here.

Dot How many houses are you going to look at, Mum? You've already looked at three.

Mum exits and can be heard offstage checking out the house.

Ethel Hey, Dot.

Dot What?

> *Dot and Ethel begin to engage the audience, and talk about them, improvising.*

Aunty Dot Hey, you girls, don't be so rude, this mob's paying good money to be here.

Dot & Ethel [*together*] Sorry, Aunty Dot.

> *Mum enters.*

Mum This is the one, start unloading.

Choosing a New House

Ethel [*narration*] Our new place wasn't the prettiest house but it was just big enough to fit the whole family, [*looking at Ruffy*] dog and all.

Mum [*talking to the dog*] Ruffy, outside if you're going to mark your territory.

Dot Ouuu… yukkk!

Ethel It smells in here.

Mum Open up the windows, let in some air.

Ethel Why did you pick this house, Mum? It's dirty.

Mum Never mind, the other one had a pretty white fence, this one's got the best stove. I'll be able to make my famous scones.

Dot Yumm. And you could make… ummm…

Ethel Dumplings with golden syrup and cream.

Dot And you could make…

Ethel Make pancakes, with lemon and sugar.

Dot What about…?

Ethel Fairy cakes with their little butterfly wings.

Dot Yeahh.

Aunty Dot Aye, you mob, you haven't even settled in yet.

Mum Once we clean it up, it will be beautiful, you'll see.

Dot Yeah.

Ethel Where are we going to sleep?

Mum We'll put the mattresses on the floor for now. When we're settled Dad can make some beds with fancy headboards.

Dot Yeahhhh, he can even make you a beautiful kitchenette.

Mum A what?

Dot A beautiful kitchenette.

Ethel Us girls can paint it a pretty pale blue.

Mum And over here a big kitchen table with stools to sit on.

Ethel Oh, Mum, I can see it already.

Dot Yeahh!

Ethel And you can make us some pretty frilly

curtains for the windows.

Mum See, it will be better in no time.

Dot Yeah!

Mum Dot, get the boys to skin the rabbit.

Dot runs offstage.

Dot [*calling as she goes*] Boys! Mum wants youse to skin the rabbit!

Ethel Which room can us girls have?

Mum Girls on the left, boys on the right. Me and Dad in the middle.

Ethel It's going to be cold tonight, isn't it, Mum?

Mum Well, we'd better get that fire started. Rabbit stew, that'll warm you up.

Ethel And some pikelets?

Dot enters.

Dot Mum, the lady next door wants to know if you want any help.

Mum tidies her hair, then shouts outside from the door.

Mum No thank you, dear. I've already got an army of workers. But thank you.

Ethel Mum.

Mrs Pivot [*offstage*] Ah well, if you need a hand, just sing out.

Ethel Mum!

Mrs Pivot [*offstage*] Oh! I'm Mrs Tilly Pivot by the way.

Mum I'm Mrs Alice Davis, nice to meet you, Mrs Pivot.

Ethel [*shouting*] Ahhh! Mum! Ruffy piddled on the floor again.

Mum is trying to ignore Ethel in the background as she is still at the door talking to Mrs Pivot.

Mum He's just excited, you know, new house and all. Now, Ruffy, outside.

This is when Mum returns inside and shouts at the dog.

Go on, get out of here, you!

Mum goes back to the door and smiles at Mrs Pivot.

Good boy.

At the New House (the past)

The sound of a rock hitting tin. Mum looks out the door.

Mum Dorothy, get in here. Dot, what are you doing?

Dot Nothing.

Mum What's in your hand?

Dot Nothing.

Mum Let me have a look.

Dot holds out her hand. It has rocks in it.

Ethel She's been throwing them at the girls next door.

Mum You what?

Dot I didn't hit them.

Mum Lucky for you. Now give 'em 'ere.

She gives Dot a slap.

Now behave yourself.

Dot Why do I have to be good all the time?

Mum We're new here, that's why, and everybody's watching. First impressions count, Dot. Do you want your dad to lose his job because his kids are misbehaving?

Dot No.

Mum You never know, you might even get to like the girls next door.

Dot No I won't.

Mum You get out to that tank stand and go wash your face and hands.

Dot Only dirty people wash!

Mum What did you say?

Dot Nuthin'.

Mum I'll show you dirty. After I've finished scrubbing those knees and elbows, you'll see dirty.

Ethel Gee, you sure were a cheeky girl, Aunty Dot.

Aunty Dot I must have been, ay?!

Dot Oooowww, you're hurting me!

Settling In (Past)

Ethel [*narration*] After dinner we'd sit by the fire and Mum and Dad would tell us kids' stories. We didn't have a wireless or anything or TV—hadn't even been thought of. So we had to make our own fun. Dad would talk about being a young stockman up north. And Mum would tell us stories about how she'd been taken away as a littl'n and where she'd grown up. Then it was time for a hot bath with water from the copper, and straight to our room to bed. Me and Dot slept foot to foot. In this case knee to knee.

Dot Gimme some blanket, I'm cold.

Ethel Stop pulling the rug.

Dot Ow, stop pinching me.

Ethel I'll make ya sleep on the floor.

Dot Will not.

Ethel Keep your feet off me, they're freezing.

[*Pause. Looking at the roof*] Dot.

Dot Yeah?

Ethel Is that a spider up there?

Dot Where?

Ethel There. Directly above us.

Dot Naaa! It's just a little piece of string.

Ethel Why would they have a piece of string up there?

Dot I don't know. Go to sleep.

Ethel is moving around in the bed and looking under it.

What ya doing?

Ethel Where's your candle?

Dot Why?

Ethel I just want to make sure.

Dot You won't find it 'cause I sold it to the boys.

Ethel For how much?

Dot Halfpenny. [Ape-knee.]

Ethel giggles.

What?

Ethel Well, they gave me a penny for mine.

Dot How come you got more money than me?

Ethel You only gave them half a candle, that's why.

Dot Well, next time I'm goin' to sell them a full one.

Ethel [*narration*] After the rest of the house had gone to sleep, I'd lay awake listening to the sounds of the night, watching the shadows dance across the wall, and snuggle into my bed knowing that I was warm and safe.

Mum [*offstage*] Time to go to sleep, you lot.

Dot & Ethel [*together*] Yes, Mum.

Mum You put that dog out.

Ethel & Dot [*together*] Yes, Mum.

Dot Shhhhhh… Ruffy.

Aunty Dot wakes up Ethel.

Aunty Dot Hey, wake up now, you got to be the teacher. Come on, Ruffy, you've got to come with me.

The School House (the past)

Knock, knock.

Teacher Come in.

Mum Excuse me.

Teacher Yes.

Mum I've come to enrol my children.

Teacher Oh. Oh. Mrs Davis, isn't it?

Mum Yes… and you are?

Teacher I'm Miss O'Connor.

Mum There are six school-age children—two girls, four boys.

Teacher Oh! Goodness.

Mum They used to go to school in Waroona.

Teacher Oh.

Mum And they can read and write.

Teacher Oh, good, that's good.

Mum So?

Teacher Well, I'd have to get approval from… the Department of Education.

Mum Don't the other mill workers' children come here?

Teacher Well. Yes. There are no other native children at this school, Mrs Davis.

Mum And…

Teacher There may be some difficulties.

Mum You won't have any difficulties with my children.

Teacher It's a small town, Mrs Davis, and some people think—rightly or wrongly—some people are not happy about having a native family here in the town, let alone taking up one of the jobs at the mill.

Mum I'll have my children here tomorrow.

Teacher I'll have to get permission from the Department.

Mum I'm sure you will. I'll see you tomorrow.

Teacher It may take some time.

Mum Well, in the meantime, you can take them on approval, until the Department sorts itself out. The sooner they start the better, don't you think?

The Teacher nods and scratches. Mum exits.

Yarloop—Looking for a School (the present)

Jude Well, here we are.

Dot Don't walk so fast. My quan's sore from sitting in that car.

Ethel How could it be sore, you made us stop ten times so you could have your smoke.

Dot What about you?! Toilet stop every twenty miles.

Ethel I can't help it, you know I got a weak bladder.

Jude Hey, between you both, you've stretched a one and a half hour trip into three hours.

Dot Come on, Ethel, get out of the car.

Ethel Don't be stupid, Dot. I'm not looking at an empty paddock.

Dot But it used to be there.

Ethel Well, it ain't there now.

Jude Go on, Ethel, we come this far. And you've eaten all the Tim Tams.

Dot Judith.

Ethel Orright, then. But if you wanted to look at a empty paddock, you didn't have to come all the way to Yarloop.

Dot That patch there is where the schoolhouse used to stand. One big room for Years One to Seven.

Ethel I reckon that's where we used to sit and eat our bread and dripping sandwiches.

Jude picks up something.

Jude Hey, this looks like a bit'a old blackboard.

Dot & Ethel [*together*] Naaa!

Ethel picks up something.

Ethel Dot, here's a souvenir for you.

Dot What? [*She has a closer look.*] Just a bloody rock.

Ethel It might be the same one you hit Jenny Mayer with.

Dot I never hit her with a rock! I used my case.

   Dot throws the rock.

Aunty Dot Aye, mind the car.

Jude You get teased, Dot?

Dot Bloody oath I did!

Ethel She used to start fights all the time.

Dot True as God, Ethel, you must have been blind. I never started the fights. They did.

Ethel No one teased me.

Dot Deaf as well as blind.

Ethel Least I've still got my memory.

Dot And what do you mean by that, you cranky old bitch.

Aunty Dot Ay, ay, ay. Settle down.

Dot Sorry, Aunty Dot.

Jude What, you talking to yourself now?

Ethel All I'm saying is that I had good friends here. I fitted in with the white kids.

Dot You thought you fitted in, Ethel. But you didn't really.

Jude Were you the only Noongar kids here?

Dot And reminded of that practically everyday.

Jude Yeah, there's a letter of complaint in the files

Dot Sssshh, Jude.

Ethel That's it! Mention those files again and you can take me back to Perth.

Jude I'm sorry. Just trying to get a picture of what it must have been like. Especially being the only Noongars here.

Ethel Mum made sure we fitted in regardless.

Dot I had a white friend. Well, for a little while, I think.

Ethel And I nearly got into a fight!

Dot No you never.

Ethel Yes I did. With you. Well, it wasn't really a fight, it was more like an argument.

Jude That doesn't sound like you two!

The school bell rings.

School Life (the past)

Dot Awwww, Mummmmm. Mummm.

Mum Hurry up or you'll be late.

Dot I can't find my shoes.

Mum They're under the bed where you left them.

Dot I think Ruffy wet them.

Mum You sure?

Dot Mum, they smell like pee.

Mum Don't worry, I'll fix that. Where's the eucalyptus?

Ethel [*narration*] For my first day at school, Mum made me this lovely dress, isn't it beautiful? See, little spots. A big wide sash. A flarey skirt. I love the way it moves when I spin. My shoes are beautiful too. Especially the straps over the top with the little beady buttons. And my first schoolcase.

Mum Ethel, who are you talking to?

Ethel No one.

Mum Well, stop admiring yourself.

Dot You'll crack the mirror.

Ethel Can't, you already have, so there.

Dot Mum, you sure my shoes smell all right?

Mum Of course, dear, good as new. [*Shouting offstage*] Jake, Thomas, Eddy, Harry, Kate, B, you lot stick together, you hear me.

Ethel [*narration*] School was great, all of us kids made friends, we just seemed to fit in, we were all equal.

Dot Can I play with you?

Ethel No.

Dot Awwwww.

Ethel Go away.

Dot Please.

Ethel Shhhh. I'll play skippy with you when we get home.

Dot Promise.

Ethel Promise.

Girl Nigger, nigger, pull the trigger.

Dot Look the other way.

Girl Nigger, nigger, pull the trigger.

Ethel Dot, where are you going?

Dot You heard what she said.

Ethel Don't worry about it.

Dot Nobody's going to call us niggers and get away with it.

Dot exits.

Ethel Dot, come back here. You know what Mum said.

The girl goes offstage.

Dot [*offstage*] Take it back.

Girl [*offstage*] No.

Dot [*offstage*] I said take it back.

Girl [*offstage*] Ow, stop pulling my hair... you

lousy nig—aahhhh!

Ethel Dot…!

Dot returns.

Dot Well… I got her a beauty. Don't think she'll be calling us names again. [*Holding up a hair ribbon*] Look.

Ethel That was in her hair.

Dot Yeah!

Ethel You better give it back and say you're sorry. You know what Mum told us! Sticks and stones.

Dot I'll break her bones.

Ethel Dot.

Dot She shouldn't of said what she said.

Ethel I'm gonna tell Mum on you.

Dot I don't care.

Dot exits.

Home After School (the past)

Ethel Mum!

Mum So how was school?

Ethel Good, Mum.

Mum Did you make any friends?

Ethel Yeah. Rebecca and Effie. Mum.

Mum How was your teacher?

Ethel Good, she made me read in front of the whole class. You should of seen her face after.

Mum You surprised her, eh?

Ethel Didn't even make one mistake.

Mum Good girl. What about Dot, how'd she go?

Ethel Oh yeah! Mum, she got into a fight.

Mum Dorothy.

Ethel Ask her where she got the ribbon.

Dot enters.

Mum Dot. Get in here. What did I tell you?

Dot But she called us niggers.

Mum What did I tell you?

Ethel Sticks and stones.

Mum Ethel.

Dot shrugs her shoulders.

Dot I don't know.

Mum Do you want to get expelled?

Dot But she started it.

Mum It doesn't matter who started it. When they say things that hurt you, just walk away… just walk away.

Letter One

To the Chief Protector of Aborigines, Perth.

With regard to question 11 on circular number 108. There are a number of children, members of this Davis family, who could, with advantage, be removed to an institution, and in my opinion should be removed in the interest of other children in the district. These children attend the state school at Yarloop and I am sure that their presence is objectionable to some people.

Constable O'Brien, 1116/1931

An Evening Outside the Pictures (the past)

Eddy Roll up, roll up, roll up. Ray's Electric Pictures on tonight. Roll up, roll up, roll up. Get in quick, don't be late. [*Narration*] The picture shows were held on Saturday nights. One of my brothers got a job as the first black town crier. Before the pictures he would be shouting and ringing his bell up and down the street. He had a gang of boys with him. And he was allowed to get one of his mates in for free.

Ethel Hi, Eddy.

Eddy What you doing here?

Ethel Can I come to the pictures with you?

Eddy Nah, I'm taking my mate.

Ethel Can Dot and I sneak in then?

Eddy You want me to lose my job?

Ethel Please, we've even got dressed up. See.

She spins around.

Eddy All right, then. If I do this [*motioning with his hand*] it's safe. If I do this [*motioning with his hand*] it's not.

Ethel Thanks, Eddy.

Eddy But you have to sit up the back and keep quiet. And don't tell nobody.

Ethel Thanks, Eddy. We won't tell anyone.

Eddy Aye, shhh.

Eddy exits.

[*Offstage, calling*] Roll up, show starts at eight. Roll up, roll up.

Ethel Dot… Dot.

Dot enters.

Dot What?

Ethel Hurry up.

Dot Is he gonna let us in?

Ethel Yeah, but we have to wait for him to give us a signal.

Dot What signal?

Ethel [*gesturing*] When he does this, we can go in.

Dot What if he doesn't?

Ethel Well, he'll get this.

    She gives the hand signal of punching.

Dot Ethel, don't make me laugh, you can't fight.

Ethel No. But you can.

The Picture Theatre (the past)

Ethel [*narration*] All of Yarloop would pile into the Town Hall, dressed to the nines. With their boxes of chocolates and bags of boiled lollies clutched tightly in their hands.

    The picture goes into 'God Save the King'. The girls try to get everyone in the audience up.

Girls [*singing*] '… God save the King…'

Ethel [*narration*] We loved to see those big Hollywood stars up there on the silver screen. Charlie Chaplin, [*ha, ha*] Tom Mix [*wooo*] and Lillian Gish [*whistle*]. Us girls imagined ourselves being carried away by Ruldoph Valentino, on his big white horse [*ahhh*]. But the boys, they loved the Westerns…

Boys [*calling out*] Here comes the cowboys, here comes the indians, here comes the cavalry.

Ethel [*narration*] After the pictures we'd be playing cowboys and indians all the way home. [*Wo/wo/wo/wo!*]

A cowboy kills an indian.

And you can guess you played the indians.

Cowboy Ow!… That hurt.

Aunty Dot kills the cowboy.

Aunty Dot But the indians won that round.

Ethel [*narration*] In the summer time we'd sit outside, under the bower shed that Dad build with his own hands. It had a great big table, stools to sit on and no matter how hot the day got, it was always cool under there. Tea time was family time. We would laugh and talk about the day we had. Mum would always have a big meal spread out. And jugs of her special home-made ginger beer. We were never short of a feed. Dad would go out hunting and bring back kangaroo, duck and parrots. So our cupboards were always full. In the winter time Dad played for the local football team, even trained and coached. Mum helped out working with the ladies' club, making scones and jam. We were the Davis family of Yarloop.

Aunty Dot There you go.

Under this narration, the song 'Pearly Shells' is sung, whilst watermelon is being handed out.

Skipping (the past)

Dot [*skipping and singing*] 'Bread and butter, marmalade, jam. What is the name of your old man? D… A… D. Dad.' Come on, faster, faster.

Ethel [*shouting*] Dad, want to come skip with us?

Mum Dad's gone roo shooting.

Dot Come on then, Mum.

Mum shakes her head and pats her stomach.

Ethel [*narration*] Oh, yeah, Mum was pregnant again.

Dot Hurry up, Ethel, it's your turn.

Ethel I can't… when the rope's moving.

Dot It's easy, just jump in.

Ethel I can't.

The rope is stopped so Ethel can start jumping without having to run in when the rope is turning.

Thank you. [*Skipping and singing*] 'I call in my very best friend.' Not you, Ruffy, get out. 'I call in my very best friend. E.S.M.E. Esme.'

Dot Esme's not here, stupid!

Ethel I know. But she's my best friend. And don't call me stupid.

Dot Well, you are, so there!

Dot runs off with the skipping rope.

Ethel Muummmm. Dot's run off with the skipping rope.

Mum Don't tell tales, Ethel.

Mum walks off.

Dot Ha, ha, ha. Can't catch me.

Ethel Dot, come back here.

Dot You want it, come get it.

Ethel When I catch you, you'll be sorry.

Dot Can't catch me for a skinny old flea.

Ethel I don't care.

Dot Where are ya going?

Ethel I'm gonna find out where Dad is.

Dot He'll be miles away by now.

Ethel I'm gonna climb the water tower and see where he is, exactly.

Dot The water tower!

Ethel Yeah.

Dot You climbed it before?

Ethel Yeah.

Dot When.

Ethel Lots of times.

Dot When?

Ethel When you weren't looking.

Dot Orright then. I'll race you.

Ethel Ahhhhhh!

The actors improvise running around.

Oh, Dot… Oh, wait for me, Dot.

Dot Come on, Ethel. Don't be a sissy.

Ethel Least I'm not a tomboy like you. Dot, oh Dot, I've got a stitch.

Dot Are you orright?

Dot runs to see if Ethel is all right. Ethel runs off laughing.

The Water Tower (the past)

Dot and Ethel are both looking up.

Dot Go on then, you first.

Ethel I'm a bit puffed at the moment.

Dot You orright? Up you go.

Ethel It's very high, isn't it?

Dot Come on, follow me.

Ethel I dunno, Dot.

Dot It's easy, come on.

Ethel [*taking one step*] It's a long way up.

Dot Just don't look down.

   The actors improvise climbing—with music.

Aunty Dot Cut it out, Wayne.

Dot Grab my hand and I'll help you up.

Ethel Oooo… ahhh.

Dot See, we're touching the sky.

Ethel Stay still, you're making it shake.

Dot You can see for miles and miles.

Ethel There's Dad.

Dot Where?

Ethel Over there. [*Shouting*] Dad!

Dot I see him. Ruffy's with him too.

Ethel He looks so small.

Dot Hey, Ruffy! Ruf, Ruf, woof, woof!

Ethel Ruffy, Ruffy! Woo, woo, woo, woo! Can we go now?

Dot No, wait until we can't see Dad no more. [*Shouting*] Dad! Dad!

Ethel He can't hear ya.

Dot [*tearing herself, shouting loudly*] Dad!

Ethel I think he might have heard that.

Dot Dad! Bring back some good tucker! Luv you… Dad!

Ethel Love you, Dad!

Late in the Evening—Outside (the past)

Mum looks through the trees and then sits down.

Ethel Mum, I can't sleep. I keep hearing this strange bird outside my window.

    Mum looks at Ethel and doesn't answer. She changes the subject.

Mum Nothing to be scared of. It's only a bird.

Ethel Shall I put Dad's dinner in the oven?

Mum He'll be home soon.

Ethel He's taking a long time. Isn't he?

Mum It's late. Go to bed. Give me a kiss.

Ethel Can you get him to tuck us in, when he comes home?

Mum Yes, Ethel.

Ethel Goodnight, Mum.

Mum Goodnight, darling.

Ethel [*narration*] When I came home from school the next day. The house was silent. Mum was sitting with her head in her hands. When I got closer I could hear her crying. It was then I knew what that bird meant.

File Note

5th of September 1932

Re: Death of William Davis—Half-Caste Aborigine.

Constable O'Brien advised by phone this morning that half-caste William Davis met with his death yesterday. Whilst out hunting. With regard to the family of Deceased, who left a wife and ten children, ages ranging from twenty years to seven months. It appears to me that something will now have to be done in connection with them. The children are in constant association with the white boys and girls of Yarloop and I do not think that it is in the best interests of either the white children or the Davis children, that this association should be permitted to continue. I am of the opinion that they should be sent some place where they will be able to mix with persons of their own race.

A.O. Neville

Chief Protector of Aborigines

The Cemetery—Yarloop (the present)

Ethel Noorn. May Bell. 1902 to 1903.

Jude She was only one, poor baby.

Ethel This one was only five.

Jude What's on his tombstone?

Ethel No tombstone. Just a number.

Jude Can you remember where?

Ethel I think it was… somewhere near a gum tree. Towards the back.

Dot Do you know which grave is his?

Ethel Don't know exactly, too long ago.

Dot What's important is that we are here.

Jude Feels like he's with us.

Dot Like his spirit is. Aye?

Ethel I remember the day it happened, Dot. We'd climbed up that bloody water tower.

Dot It was the last time we ever saw him.

Ethel He turned and faced us. His hand raised above his head.

Dot I waved that little hanky till he disappeared from sight.

Ethel Yarloop was never the same after that.

Dot Dad was out hunting when it happened, Jude, crossing old George's paddock. This bloody bull chased him. He tripped, fell, broke his neck. For years afterwards, I'd lay on my bed with my hand over my ears and hear that roaring and running. But it was only the beat of my heart, thumping through my eardrums.

Jude You right, sis?

Dot Yeah, I'm fine.

Ethel This is the first time we've been back since it happened.

Dot We came with Mum by horse and cart. This time we came in a flash car.

Ethel She was the last one to place a flower on the grave.

Dot She just stood looking down, not saying anything.

Ethel First time I saw her cry like that.

Aunty Dot After Dad died, the struggle really began. It was the middle of the Depression. While the whitefellas got what was called sustenance, us blackfellas got rations.

Letter Two

To Chief Protector, Aborigines Department,

Mr Neville.

Dear Sir,

I wish to rectify my mistake that I was receiving one pound sustenance instead of saying rations. As it is I do not get as much as one pound. I receive fifteen shillings and eight pence in groceries and three shillings and eleven pence in meat. I don't see why I should be treated any different than the rest of the people here as I have to vote and am expected to do as the white people do. Surely, Mr Neville, it is little enough I am asking for as I have had a hard struggle to keep the little one without saying anything for the big boys. Mr Davis has been killed five months and I have struggled on but it is quite impossible to do any longer as we are all in need of such a lot.

Hoping this letter meets with your approval.

Yours humbly,

Alice Davis.

Letter Three

Mrs A. Davis,

I acknowledge receipt of your letter of the 28th. I am now awaiting a report from my investigating officer at Yarloop as to your actual circumstances and when this is received I shall come to a decision in the matter. But I am afraid on the particulars now before me that it will be necessary to discontinue the rations which you now obtain from this department.

Yours faithfully,

Chief Protector of Aborigines.

3rd of February 1933.

A Government Worker Visits (the past)

Ethel [*narration*] One day a man in a suit arrived at our front door. This was the visit Mum had been fearing for a long time. He was from the Department of Native Welfare. He stood on the porch and told Mum that the company that Dad had worked for, for the last seven years, had sent notification for us to vacate our home in Yarloop. And he said that it was the opinion of Mr A.O. Neville that us children be put in the care of Native Welfare and be sent to a mission. Mum said over her dead body and told him to get moving out of our yard.

Mum And you can tell Mr Neville he might be your boss, but he ain't mine.

Leaving Yarloop (the past)

Ethel You sure told him.

Dot Mum, what did that man want?

Mum Get all the kids together.

Dot Why, Mum?

Mum We're leaving, that's why.

Ethel Where are we going?

Mum Get everyone to grab what you can. [*Pause.*] What are you both still standing there for? Go, now!

Dot What's wrong?

Ethel Where are we going?

Dot Mum.

Ethel Where are we going?

Mum As long as I've got these pair of hands, nobody's going to take my babies away.

Ethel Where do they want to take us, Mum? What have we done?

Mum Ethel, rug up baby Jude, and put her things together.

Dot I'll go find Ruffy. Ruffy!

Mum Don't worry about him, Dot.

Dot Where's his lead?

Ethel What's going to happen, Mum?

Mum We'll be all right.

Dot [*calling*] Ruffy, Ruffy!

Mum We can't take him, Dot.

Dot Yes, we can.

Mum Dorothy. Come here. Now listen to me. We've got a long way to go. I don't know what's going to happen. We can't take him with us.

Dot But he's family.

Ethel We'll all look after him, Mum.

Mum No.

Dot But, Mum, please. I'll keep him quiet, Mum.

Mum I said no.

   Music. Dot cries.

[*Calling offstage*] Come on, Dot! We're going!

Dot [*crying, holding Ruffy's lead*] Ruffy.

END OF ACT ONE

ACT TWO

Brookton (the present)

Aunty Dot Brookton.

Dot Ethel, get off the track before you get hit by a train.

Ethel No train coming.

Jude What you looking for?

Dot You won't find any coal. They use diesel now.

Ethel Mum's wedding ring.

Dot Hah! That was over sixty years ago.

Ethel Well, you never know it might still be here.

Dot You won't find it, Ethel! It fell down the toilet of a moving train. It could be anywhere.

Ethel Here, give me a hand up. [*She gets onto the platform.*] We slept here, remember, Dot? No bench, just a bare floor.

Dot Didn't look like this when we came from Yarloop. It looks smaller now, unna?

Jude Nah, it's just because you're bigger.

Dot Well, you're certainly bigger. You were just a little coolunga. [baby]

Ethel We had to carry you everywhere.

Jude And I was such a beautiful baby, unna.

Aunty Dot Naah, you were just an ordinary black kid.

Ethel Mum took us to the station that night, eh Dot, brought us all tickets for Brookton and then we—

Dot Nah, nah, nah. That's not what happened. This is how the real story goes—

Ethel Dot, you wouldn't know, you were too little.

Dot Was not. I was with Mum when she gave Mrs Pivot all the money from her special jar to buy tickets for us and then we—

Ethel Well, I don't remember that happening.

Dot Why don't you just get back and look for that wedding ring.

Ethel No need to get smart.

Dot I'll tell Jude what really happened.

Ethel You? I'm the one telling the story.

Dot Go back to Yarloop, that's your town. Brookton's mine.

Ethel Since when?

Dot Since now!

Ethel Well, if Miss Brookton Reserve 1935 wants to tell the story then go right ahead. I'm gonna have a look in this art and craft shop. Might even buy a map so I can find my way round. If we're relyin' on your memory, at least I won't get lost.

Ethel exits.

Jude Ethel.

Dot You gotta have the last word, unna?

Jude Ethel.

Aunty Dot Never mind the last word, you're only supposed to be acting, you know.

A transition into the past.

Dot [*narration*] Mum got Tilly Pivot from next door to buy train tickets for us. She didn't want the police to know where we were going. She didn't even tell us kids in case we told our friends. Our older brothers had gone up north to find work. That left Mum, us five girls and our younger brother Freddy. Mum sat staring out the window, rocking baby Jude. Us bigger kids squeezed together. None of us really slept except baby Jude. And the train ride seemed to go on forever. When we reached Brookton it was still night time.

Arrival at Brookton (the past)

Ethel Where are we?

Mum Brookton.

Dot It's dark.

Mum Stay close. I don't want you falling on the tracks.

Dot I can't see.

Mum Feel your way, and watch where you're stepping.

Ethel It's cold.

Dot Where are we going?

Ethel Mum, do you know where we're going?

Mum Follow me. We'll put our things in this room here and sleep until daybreak.

The First Day in Brookton (the past)

Dot [*narration*] In the half light of dawn I opened my eyes and all I could see was this shadowy figure coming towards us. True as God, I swore it was a ghost. But it was only the station master. He made us a billy of tea, then gave directions to the nearest camp.

Ethel Hey, wait for me.

Aunty Dot We thought nobody knew we left Yarloop. But Native Welfare kept track of us. Too right, that bloody station master made sure of that. He must've run so fast down to that cop shop, probably passed himself twice on the way.

Dot [*narration*] We picked up our belongings and

started the long journey out of town. It seemed like we were going to walk forever.

Ethel Gee, my feet are sore.

Dot So are mine.

Mum Stop thinking about it and it won't bother you.

Dot How much further?

Mum Not far.

Ethel Not far? Not far to where?

Mum I don't want to hear anymore.

Dot [*narration*] When we finally stopped it seemed like the middle of nowhere.

Mum You lot wait here and don't get into any mischief.

Mum walks on ahead.

Aunty Dot Mischief! Didn't have the energy to get up to any mischief. We were just happy to sit and rest our sore poor feet.

Dot Ethel, look at those people over there.

Dot & Ethel [*together*] They're black!

Dot Yeah. Ethel, look at them tin shacks.

Ethel Yeah.

Dot I think they live in them, Ethel.

Ethel Yeah.

Dot Are we going to live in one them?

Ethel No, no, no, we're going to live in a house.

Dot I don't see any.

Ethel Mum's just asking for directions.

Dot You sure?

Ethel Yeah. See, she's asking that lady.

Dot How far away do you reckon the houses are?

Ethel Not too far I hope, my feet are killing me.

   Mum returns.

Mum Come on, you lot, start unpacking.

Dot What, here?

Mum This is where we're staying tonight.

Ethel But it's just the ground!

Mum Shhh, Ethel. Sleeping on the ground won't kill you! You can see who can count the most stars before you fall asleep. And if you look real hard, you'll see the emu in its nest.

Ethel I'm not sleeping in the dirt.

Mum You'll sleep where I tell you.

Dot [*narration*] We had dinner that night with Aunty Maude, Mum's tribal sister, who welcomed us with open arms. We had ashes damper and kangaroo stew. Us kids sat quietly and ate while the older people talked. Back in Yarloop, Mum never talked about her childhood up north. She was taken from her family when she was only four years old. And put into a mission. That's where she met Aunty Maude. They were both taken from there to a homestead where they had to do domestic service. They swore as children they would always look out for each other. Now that Dad was gone, she was the only person Mum trusted in the world. Later that night we slept on the ground all huddled around the fire. The sounds of the bush kept me awake. And we were covered with a blanket of stars.

The Next Day (the past)

Mum Come on, come on, wake up, you girls, I want you to go get some water.

Dot What, now?

Ethel It's too cold.

Mum Have a wash too, that'll freshen you up.

Dot Come on, Ethel.

Mum And I'll get breakfast started.

Ethel Where's the tap?

Mum The waterhole is over there through the trees. Follow the path.

Dot What do we carry it in?

Mum Take that tin and that stick over there.

Ethel What's the stick for?

Dot Snakes?

Ethel Oh, Mummm.

Mum No, silly. It's to hang the tin on. So you'll be able to carry the weight of the water.

Dot I knew that.

Ethel Well, come on, great water carrier of all time.

Dot Come on.

The girls head off for the waterhole.

Ethel Wait for me.

Dot Do you think we'll live here forever?

Ethel I don't know.

Dot I miss Ruffy.

Ethel I miss Ruffy too.

Dot Do you miss our house?

Ethel Yeah.

Dot I don't.

Ethel One day we'll have a new house. With our own big rooms!

Dot Big brass beds.

Ethel With real white sheets.

Dot Soft feather mattresses.

Ethel With sun steaming in, through frilly curtains.

Ethel And a big bathtub with lovely hot water.

Dot Yeahhh, Ethel. Fat chance.

At the Waterhole (the past)

Ethel Oh, oh! Dot, look! Over there.

Dot Boys!

Ethel They're blue black!

Dot All over.

> *Dot starts shooting rocks at the boys with her ging (shanghai).*

Ethel No, Dot, don't.

Dot Missed.

Ethel Dot, Dot, put it away, put it away, put it away.

> *Dot hides the ging behind her back.*

Boy Need any help with the water?

Dot & Ethel [*together*] No thanks.

Boy You sure about that?

Ethel We're not allowed to talk to strangers.

Boy Aye, you're the only strangers around here, yer uppity black gins.

Dot We're not the black gins, you are.

Boy I'm what?! [*He looks to the other boys.*] Hey, you fellas, she reckons I'm a black gin.

The boy kicks the water can.

Dot Go away, you're going to spill it.

Boy Go away, you're gonna spill it.

Dot Yeah! I'll spill you.

Dot raises her stick to hit the boy.

Ethel Dot… put that stick down.

Boy Yeah, put it down, Dot. Or I'll 'urt ya black gin sister.

Ethel Dot, put it down, put it down, put it down.

Boy Put it down, put it down, put it down.

The boy grabs Ethel's hair.

Ethel Dot, pick it up, pick it up, pick it up.

Dot picks up the stick.

Hit him!

Dot goes to hit the boy who runs out of reach and shouts back, then exits.

Dot [*shouting*] I'll get you next time!

Boy [*offstage, shouting*] Nahh, I'll get you! Next time ya come for water!

Dot [*shouting*] No, I'm gonna get you, you black gin! Go' on, get!

The boy laughs loudly. Dot gets her ging out again.

Ethel No, Dot. We don't want any trouble.

Dot You orright, sis?

Ethel I don't know, have a look.

Dot You're all right, no blood.

Ethel You sure?

Dot Yeah. I'm gonna get him and I'm gonna get him good.

Ethel No, please don't, Dot.

Back from the Waterhole (the past)

The girls return with water.

Mum What took you so long?

Dot There were these smelly boys—

Ethel Dot.

Dot And they were calling us uppity black gins.

Mum Watch your mouth!

Dot But, Mum, they were.

Mum [*talking to the girls*] How many times do I have to tell you girls—walk away, remember, just walk away.

She pauses, then walks looking towards where the boys are.

[*To the girls*] Where are those boys?

The girls point in the direction of the boys.

[*Shouting off*] We don't want any trouble here, but you lot leave my girls alone!

Ethel See the trouble you've started, Dot, we're only here for one lousy day and you 'ave to start a war with the natives!

Dot Shut up, you goody-two-shoes.

Ethel Just walk away.

Letter Five

To the Chief Protect of Aborigines, Perth.

I am writing to inform you that Mrs Davis and family have moved to Brookton from Yarloop. I inspected the camps last Thursday and noticed they were not with the others but have a camp on the main road to Pingelly. A kerosene tin humpy has been erected. Water at the new camp will be difficult, there is plenty of water, but it appears to be going brackish.

Yours sincerely,

Constable Hess.

Our House (the past)

Dot [*narration*] Our new home was made out of blackboy rushes and old flattened-out kerosene tins. We had to make do with what we could, so Mum spread out woggas made of wheat bags and covered them with bullrushes to make a bed on the ground. No flash stove like Yarloop. Just damper in the ashes and billy tea. Every morning Mum would leave us kids at the camp and walk the long miles into town looking for work.

Ethel If Mum gets a job, she might bring us back some humbugs.

Dot You've been saying that every day.

Ethel She'll find one soon.

Dot Wanna go down to the creek?

Ethel Mum said we gotta stay close to the camp. [*Pause.*] Aye, Dot. Look here!

Dot What?

Ethel Is that a snake track, going into our house?

Dot That's a snake track all right. Big one too!

Ethel You sure it's a snake?

Dot Yep.

Ethel Couldn't be a lizard?

Dot Ethel! Lizards got legs.

Ethel Well, see if the track comes out the other side.

Dot Nothing! Must still be in there.

Ethel We'd better wait for Mum.

Dot What if it's too dark when she gets back? We'll have to sleep outside.

Ethel ponders the situation. She looks to Aunty Dot who shows her what to do. Ethel picks up a big stick and gives it to Dot.

Ethel Well! Seeing I'm the oldest. You should do it.

Dot Why me?

Ethel 'Cause you run faster.

Dot What do I do when I find it?

Ethel Hit it on the head and kill it.

Dot enters the house.

Hey, Dot.

Dot Yeah?

Ethel See him yet?

Dot No. Ahhhh! It is a bloody big bastard!

Ethel Hit him.

Dot I am. You take that… and that and that!

Silence.

Ethel [*whispering*] Dot… [*Louder*] Dot… [*Shouting*] Dot!

Dot Yeah, what?

Ethel You got it?

Dot [*walking out with the snake*] Yep.

Ethel Sure it's dead?

Dot Here… look.

Dot chases Ethel with the snake. Ethel screams. Mum enters.

Mum Aye, aye, aye. What's going on here?

Dot I killed a snake, Mum, look.

Mum You what?

Dot It was under our blankets.

Mum You could of got killed.

She gives Dot a slap.

You should've waited till I got home.

Dot We didn't know how long you were going to be.

Mum It doesn't matter.

Dot But, but, but, what if it got dark, and we had sleep outside?

Mum And what if you got bit?

Ethel Yeah.

Mum Ethel, why did let your little sister go in there?

She gives Ethel a slap.

You're supposed to be the eldest.

Both girls are uspet from being slapped.

Ethel I tried to stop her, Mum, but Dot just took off in there.

Dot You said because you were the oldest, I should go in.

Pause.

Ethel Did you bring any humbugs?

Mum No.

Dot You find some work?

Mum Something will turn up.

Dot What we gonna have for supper?

Mum There's enough flour for a damper.

Dot Is there anything else?

Ethel We got some dripping.

Mum I tell you what, I'll show you how to cook snake.

Dot Yeah!

Ethel Snake. Mum it's poisonous.

Mum No. You cut out the poison.

Dot Did you do that in the olden days?

Mum Yeah, the old fellas on the station showed me how to. See… look here… you just cut off the head.

Ethel We're all gonna die!

Mum See… this is where the poison is… here. And you just throw this bit away.

Ethel Yukk!

Mum Ethel. It's meat, like anything else. Up north, where I come from, snake is good tucker.

Ethel Well, I'm not eatin' it.

Mum It just tastes like chicken.

Aunty Dot Everything tastes like chicken, unna.

Dot I'll try some. Just a little bit.

Ethel You can have my bit.

Mum Ethel, you make the damper.

Ethel Orright.

Aunty Dot Hey, Eth. Here's one I prepared earlier.

Music improvisation.

Aunty Dot sits with the others, and gets the damper out of ashes. While she is doing this, Mum gets the billy, Ethel grabs the cups. Tea is poured and damper shared around amongst the actors, and Aunty Dot and Uncle Frankie. Music is playing in background. Mum then gets up and offers damper to the audience.

Brookton—Police Station (the present)

Ethel See that big white gum tree across the road. That's where all the blackfellas used to sit on ration day, waiting for the constable to call out their name.

Dot These windows used to have bars on them.

Jude Aye, you fellas, look at all these Noongar names scratched on the walls here.

Dot Choo, had to leave their mark for everyone to see.

Ethel No shame in a Noongar scratching his mark on a prison door.

Dot Better than scratching something else. If you weren't out of town by six o'clock you'd wind up in here.

Jude With one hand they're feeding ya food, and with the other they lockin' ya up.

Aunty Dot Too true.

Dot That's true, it was so they could keep an eye on everyone.

Ethel Used to walk miles just to sit and wait over there for our little bit of flour, tea and sugar.

Dot Blistered feet and empty bellies, that's all we got.

Ethel Hardly ever got fresh meat. Or milk.

Dot True, ey.

Ethel Mum was worried about losing you, Jude. You were only a baby and she had no milk.

Dot That stinkin' water made you crook.

Jude True.

Ethel I can remember her sitting up writing to Native Welfare.

Dot That wasn't an easy thing for her to do either. She had to swallow her pride.

Jude I saw that letter in the file somewhere.

Dot Well, that's the end of this trip!

The following letters allow a transition into the past.

Letter Six

Dear Chief Protector,

I am writing to ask if you will let me have some milk for my baby. She cannot be expected to survive on flour and tea alone. Could you also supply me with a bar of soap to wash the kiddies and some meat. After all, we are only human the same as your own.

Yours sincerely,

Mrs A. Davis.

Letter Seven

Mrs Davis,

I have asked Constable Hess to supply you with soap. In regard to your other requests, the trouble is, if you get it, they will all want it. And I have been informed that there are plenty of rabbits to be had for the catching.

Yours sincerely,

A.O. Neville, Chief Protector.

At the Camp (the past)

Mum I need you girls to help out more.

Ethel What do you want us to do, Mum?

Dot Anything, it's so boring around here.

Mum Good. Tomorrow I want you to go pickin' wool.

Dot Yeah, we'll do it!

Ethel Mum! That's stinkin' hard work!

Dot What's so hard about it?

Ethel You got to pick wool off maggoty dead sheep, Dot.

Dot Oooo… yukkk!

Ethel Yeah, yukk.

Mum We'll get good money for it. We can sell it when the wool buyer comes to town. Just don't let the farmers catch you.

Dot Isn't there anything else we could do?

Mum Yes. Get some manna gum, and we need more wood, and you can keep an eye out for rabbits.

Aunty Dot You won't have time to be bored now!

Mum As long as we all pitch in, we'll get along fine. You're young women now.

Rabbit Huntin' (the past)

Dot None in this one.

Ethel None in this one.

Dot Bloody foxes!

Ethel Bloody foxes! Got this sweet little bunny before we did.

Dot So what are we going to try this time?

Ethel Chase 'em or dig 'em?

Dot Dig 'em.

Ethel Ohh… Where there's a will, there's a way.

The 'Run Rabbit' song.

Dot [*referring to a rabbit hole*] Hey, Ethel, here's one. Fresh one.

Ethel Yeah.

Dot Look for another hole.

Ethel & Dot [*together*] There it is.

Ethel I saw it first. Any more fresh ones?

Dot No. Just get over there and I'll start digging.

Ethel looks around.

Ethel Orright… I'm waiting.

Dot digs in hole.

Dot I feel something… Hey, he's moving! Hey, get ready, he's comin'!

Ethel Where?

Dot Just get ready.

Ethel I'm ready… I'm ready.

Dot looks up.

Dot Ohhh, Ethel.

Ethel What?

Dot You let him get away.

Ethel What?

Dot At the other hole.

Ethel What other hole?

Dot You're at the wrong hole!

Ethel What?

Both girls stand looking at each other.

What you looking at me like that for?

Dot That was supper.

Ethel Wasn't my fault, you told me to stand here?

Dot Don't matter whose fault it is. We're gonna go hungry again.

Ethel Just walk away.

Dot [*narration*] On the weekends we'd go to town. Mum had a special money jar, that no one was allowed to touch. Any money that anyone made she'd put it in there. If we were good and made a bit of extra money from the jobs we'd done, Mum would let us have a threepence each to buy sweets.

Ethel What are you gonna buy?

Dot Humbugs, spearmint leaves, liquorice, jubes, boiled lollies, penny sticks, love hearts.

Ethel I'm savin' mine.

Dot Hey, Eth, look at that Malvern Star bike.

Ethel takes no notice.

Ethel [*to herself*] Look at the man on the bike.

Dot I'm talking about what he's sitting on.

Ethel So am I. He's good-lookin', bit too good-lookin' if you ask me.

Dot What, him? He's a footy player from Pingelly Districts.

Ethel Do you know him?

Dot Saw him play last Sunday.

Ethel Didn't you go to Sunday School?

Dot He sent that footy right down the middle.

Ethel What's his name?

Dot Dunno.

Ethel Go find out his name and I won't tell on you.

Dot Wadda ya mean tell on me?

Ethel Wagging church, missy.

Dot How much money did Mum give us?

Ethel A threepence each, why?

Dot Gimme yours and I'll find out his name for ya.

Ethel I'll give you a penny.

Dot exits.

Dot [*shouting*] Hey, Eth. His name is Giddeon Bennell.

Ethel Dot, what ya shout like that for? Did ya have to tell the whole world?

Dot Never told the whole world. Just you and all his footy mates.

Ethel God, Dot. I've never been so embarrassed in my whole life.

Dot Look, he's comin' over to see ya.

Ethel Come on, let's get goin'.

Dot No, he's comin'.

Ethel I'm not gonna see him now.

Dot Too late, now. You can run, but ya can't hide.

Ethel You just want to have a ride on his bike.

Dot Yeah. And you just want to have a—

Giddeon enters with his bike.

Giddeon Gidday. Ya sister said ya wanted to see me.

Ethel Hello. You know what little sisters are like, always tellin' lies. She just wanted an excuse to ride your bike.

Giddeon She can have a ride… if she wants.

Dot Thanks, Giddeon.

Dot exits with the bike, and a big smile.

Ethel Now you've done it, you'll have a hard time gettin' it off her.

Giddeon Oh, well. Just have to talk to you then.

Ethel So.

Giddeon So. What ya come to town for?

Ethel Nothing.

Giddeon You gonna come watch me play footy?

Ethel Maybe.

Giddeon Did ya see me play last weekend?

Ethel Yeah, you sent that ball right through the middle.

Giddeon Oh, yeah.

Dot re-enters on the bike.

Dot Hey, you two, what ya doin'?

Dot exits again.

Ethel Dot, don't be silly, ya might fall.

Giddeon Nah, she'll be orright.

Ethel How long you had ya bike?

Giddeon Not long.

Ethel Must 'ave cost a lot?

Giddeon Had to save for ages.

Ethel It's a nice bike.

Dot re-enters on the bike.

Dot Aye, Ethel. Look.

She exits again.

Giddeon Ever ridden?

Ethel No.

Giddeon Suppose I'll have to teach ya, then?

Ethel I dunno.

Giddeon Could take ya for a dinky, one time.

Ethel Maybe.

Giddeon Well, I better get goin', got to play soon—

> *Dot crosses the stage again on the bike.*

Ethel Hey, Dot, come back here with that bike. Giddeon's gotta go.

Dot Come and get it.

Giddeon Can I ask ya something?

Ethel Suppose.

Giddeon Want to come to the Pingelly Show with me?

Ethel Maybe.

Giddeon I'll take that as a yes, then?

Ethel We'll see. Mr Giddeon Bennell.

Dot [*narration*] The Pingelly Show would come around once a year. We would 'ave to find ways of getting there. Pingelly was about twelve miles from Brookton. It was really a meeting place for all the Noongars. At night there'd be dances, and a lot of romance going on in the bushes.

Dot [*joking about the romancing going on in the bushes*] Hey, Ethel, what's them twigs doin' in your hair?

Ethel Aww…

Dot [*narration*] There'd be two-up games and boxing tents and a sideshow alley with its kewpie dolls and knock-'em-downs.

Giddeon Step right up and have go. Otherwise you'll never know. Don't be shy, just close your eyes, 'cause every winner gets a prize.

The actors improvise a few knock-'em-down games. Dot give out prizes of toffee apples.

Dot Let's give a hand to our Magical Music Men. Uncle Frankie J. Bropho and his little white cousin Wayne. [*Narration*] And baby Jude was walking now, and singing and dancin' too. Mum entered Jude in the big tent talent quest.

The Lollipop Scene (the past)

Jude sings a few bars from 'The Good Ship Lollypop'.

Dot And the kewpie doll prize goes to the black Shirley Temple, Miss Judy Davis. [*Narration*] Yeah, we loved them Hollywood stars orright. That old dust would be fairly flying, the piano accordion playing. And them old fellas on the mouth organ.

Ethel Aunty Dot, what dances did you used to do?

The actors improvise dancing. Uncle Frankie and Aunty Dot do the barn dance. The girls follow.

Aunty Dot Well, let me show you…

Aunty Dot does the Charleston. Uncle Frankie does a dance. Everyone ends up in a choreographed dance scene.

Dot [*narration*] We'd travel home the next day, some people on horse and cart, and boys with their girls on their Malvern Star bikes. But the spirit of the show would follow us back to Brookton.

Brookton Reserve—Two-Up Night (the past)

Frankie Put your bets on, come in with your lips shakin'.

Mum I'll bet him two bob he tails it. Here, Dot, chuck it in the ring.

Aunty Dot All bets are closed. Come in, spinner.

Aunty Dot leads Uncle Frankie to throw the pennies.

Dot Arggh! Heads again!

Ethel Mum.

Mum Someone change the bloody pennies.

Frankie You think you can do better.

Mum No good betting on a crooked game!

Frankie [*throwing the pennies*] Then go and find them yourself.

Dot Aye!

Mum Choo, shame on ya. Go on, get, you rotten old crook.

Aunty Dot Rotten old crook.

Ethel I need to speak to you, Mum.

Mum Rotten old crook.

Ethel Mum, it's important.

Mum Hey, Giddeon, what are you standing back there for? Come and have a spin for me.

Ethel Forget the two-up, Mum! I need to talk to you first.

Mum Go get him, he's a good spinner.

Dot Mum! Judy's up on that forty-four-gallon drum fairly dancin'.

Mum Get her off, before she hurts herself.

Dot Jude's a real black Shirley Temple all right.

Mum Oh, no! Not that lollypop song again.

Ethel Mum.

Mum All right, Eth, what's up?

Ethel I'm leaving, Mum.

Mum What do you mean, you're leaving?

Ethel Giddeon's asked me to marry him.

Mum Mr Malvern Star, eh?

Ethel Yeah.

Mum No need to rush these things.

Ethel Mum, we've been going out for ages.

Mum You're still young, Ethel.

Ethel Mum, I'm old enough.

Mum How ya gonna live?

Ethel Giddeon's got a good job in Pingelly, working on a farm.

Mum My little girl… Ethel.

Ethel Look at it this way, it will be one less mouth to feed. You'll manage, Mum, you always do.

Mum You've made up your mind then.

Ethel We'll come visit you on weekends.

Dot re-enters.

Dot Who we going to visit on weekends?

Mum Dot. Your sister's getting married.

Dot Are ya?

Mum She's a woman now, she'll be making a new life for herself.

Brookton Reserve—Helping Mum (the past)

Dot [*narration*] Ethel married Giddeon at the Brookton Methodist Church. It was hard not having my big sister around, but Mum said it didn't matter where Ethel went, she was still part of the family. And I just had to help out a bit more. I was the eldest now.

Mum goes to pick up a rug and Dot grabs it for her.

[*To Mum*] Mum, leave that washing, I'll do it.

Mum There's not much more to do.

Dot You've been doing washing all day, look at your hands!

Mum Stop fussing, Dot, I'm orright. It's just a bit of rheumatism, that's all.

Dot You got to slow down, let us kids do more.

Mum No, Dot, it's enough that you're looking after everything while I'm at work. [*She pulls out some coins.*] Here, put this in the jar.

Brookton Reserve—The Dust Storm (the past)

Dot [*narration*] Mum still had her special savings jar that she'd been keeping all these years. We didn't know how soon we were gonna need it.

Mum Dot, get the clothes off the line.

Dot But they're not dry yet.

Mum Dust storm's coming. Grab everything.

Dot Where's Baby Jude?

76

Mum Oh God, Dot, I told you to keep an eye on her!

Dot She's with Aunty Maude.

Mum Oh, she'll be safe there.

Dot Mum, hurry, put the fire out.

Mum I'm comin'.

Dot Listen to the tin flyin'.

Mum Just get under cover.

Dot Look at the dust!

Mum We'll be orright. Just start praying!

Dot Mum, I'm scared. It's gonna blow our house down!

Mum Quick, grab the ends, hold it up!

Dot The corner is going to collapse!

Mum Use your weight, push against it!

Dot Mum I'm scared!

Mum Stick to it, girl!

Dot I can't hold it much longer!

Mum Keep pushing!

The sound of the storm dies down and they slowly walk the stage inspecting the damage.

Jesus Christ, we were lucky.

Dot Lucky? Our things could be scattered for miles. Take us months to build again.

Mum I'm not building again, Dot.

Dot What are we going to do?

Mum See if we can find that jar.

Brookton Reserve—After the Dust (the past)

A knock on the door.

Mum Mrs Crawford.

Woman Oh, hello Alice.

Mum I hear you might have a place to rent?

Woman Oh, we haven't decided what to do with it yet.

Mum I wouldn't be asking. Only we've got nowhere to go. The dust storm's taken everything.

Woman I'm so sorry, Alice.

Mum I want a real home. My children need a real home.

Woman I'll have to speak to my husband.

Mum How many years have I worked for you?

Woman A few years now.

Mum You've gotten to know me and my family.

Woman Of course, and we've become good friends.

Mum And I'm asking as a friend.

Woman Would you be able to manage the rent?

Mum Yes.

Woman I'll let you have it for three months and see how it goes.

Mum You won't be sorry.

Woman Any complaints or problems, we might have to reconsider.

Mum There won't be any problems.

Woman Just pay the rent on time.

Mum Thank you.

Letter Eight

Dear Constable Hess,

I fail to see how the local whites can object to the Davis family renting a house, after all they have not broken any law. But perhaps the trouble is over-crowding. Ten people in three small rooms does not sound too good, and this matter should be raised with the local Board of Health. With regard to the children still at home, their welfare is of some concern. I understand the mother now works and would have difficulty tending to their needs. If this is the case then the younger children would be better off at Carrolup Mission.

Yours sincerely,

A.O. Neville, Chief Protector.

Brookton—At the House (the present)

Ethel Mum, got your message, came as soon as I could.

Mum I was getting worried that you hadn't got it.

Ethel What's wrong?

Mum Where's Giddeon?

Ethel Playing footy, he'll pick me up after the game.

Mum It's about Judy.

Ethel What's happened?

Mum Nothing's happened. They reckon I'm not looking after her and threatened to take her away from me, Ethel.

Ethel Who has?

Mum Who do you think? The Department of Native Welfare.

Ethel They can't do that!

Mum Yes they can. People have complained about me having a house in town.

Ethel That's not against the law, Mum.

Mum That's right. So they think they can get me out by saying I'm neglecting my children, because I'm working.

Ethel They never worried about that when we were on the Reserve.

Mum They're trying to get me to move back there. They're trying to take my baby away, she's only four years old. It's like history repeating itself. It happened to me, but it ain't gonna happen to her.

Ethel What can I do, Mum?

Mum I want you and Giddeon to take Jude with you to Pingelly.

Ethel Oh, Mum, what about you?

Mum I'll be all right.

Ethel How you gonna live without her?

Mum As long as Jude is safe. You gotta take her. You've got to take her, Ethel!

Ethel It's all right, it's all right.

Mum We've got to keep the family together.

Ethel I won't let you down. Where is she now?

Mum Dot took her up to the Reserve to play with the kids.

Ethel Is that a good idea?

Mum She's safer there than here. Those old fellas

treat her like their own. You'll find her at Mavis's camp.

Ethel I'll get her now. Bring her back here.

Mum No.

Ethel What!

Mum Take her things with you.

Ethel Don't you want to say goodbye?

Mum You just tell her she's my baby and I love her, and I'll see her soon.

Letters to Mum from the Girls

Each of the characters speaks the letters as dia-logue to the audience.

Jude [*narration*] Dear Mother,

Hello, how are you? I am having a great time on the farm. We go into town on the weekends to the movies. I just love Jeanette McDonald. I am doing real good at school, I came first in all my races.

Can't wait for the holidays to start so I can come and stay with you. Ethel wants me to join the Girl Guides. I don't know, but.

I must close, Mum, I have to go to the shop for Ethel.

Love you, Mum.

Your loving girl, Judy.

Dot [*narration*] Dear Mum,

I hope this letter finds you in the best of health as it leaves me.

Did you get those dresses I sent you? The reason for this letter, Mum, is that the people I work for are moving to Perth and have asked me to go with them. If I don't like the big smoke I can find work back here in Wagin. They will give me a good reference if I choose to go back to the bush.

How's all them Noongars on the Reserve. Do you see them much? Are they still letting them pennies fly? Give my regards to them if you see them. I will write to you next week and let you know when I leave for Perth.

Your loving daughter, Dot.

Ethel [*narration*] Dear Mum,

How are you? Me and Gideon and the kids are happy and healthy. We went to visit Evelynn on the weekend, it was a lovely day. On the way home from her place this old Christian lady was calling out to us over the fence. I went to see what she wanted and she gave me a tin of Sunshine milk. I thought it was gonna be dripping. Before she called out, we had just scraped up a few pennies for a tin of Nestle's milk. One shilling and threepence. The kids were all pleased and one of them said God must of known we needed milk,

Mum. I let them have the money for sweets. We may be able to come and visit next weekend.

Well, Mother dear, I must close now.

Your loving daughter, Ethel.

Mother's Death—At the Cemetery (the present)

The light dims and shines on Dot.

Dot [*narration*] I was living in Wagin when I heard the bird call. I knew something was wrong so I packed up my bags and was going to see her that night. But it was too late.

The light shines on Judy.

Jude [*narration*] I wasn't allowed to go. I was too young. So I stood getting warmed by the fire. Some of Mum's friends were standing with me crying. A mass of people streamed by in silence following the hearse. When I saw that, I wanted to be alone, so I ran away to be by myself and shed tears for my mother, in my own way saying goodbye to her.

The light shines on Ethel.

Ethel [*narration*] The day I heard that Mum had her accident, it was like the memories of the past years flashed before my eyes. Yet another loved one. Mum was on the back of a horse and cart when the horse bolted. She tried to jump free, but got caught somehow. The horse was going fast and she was thrown. Uncanny really—like Dad, she had broken her neck. Mum never came to. She slipped into a coma and passed away.

At the Grave (the present)

Dot This is the one, in line with this tree.

Jude I'd hate to think what might have been if she hadn't taken us on that train to Brookton.

Ethel We're still family, Jude, that's all she wanted.

Aunty Dot Listen to the birds singing.

THE END

www.currency.com.au

Visit Currency Press' website now to:

- Buy your books online
- Browse through our full list of titles, from plays to screenplays, books on theatre, film and music, and more
- Choose a play for your school or amateur performance group by cast size and gender
- Obtain information about performance rights
- Find out about theatre productions and other performing arts news across Australia
- For students, read our study guides
- For teachers, access syllabus and other relevant information
- Sign up for our email newsletter

The performing arts publisher